Picture Credits
t=top, tr=top right, tl=top left, bl= bottom left, br=bottom right, b=bottom, m=middle,
ml=middle left, mr=middle right

Front Cover Images:

P9: Victor9876 (tr); P9: Chester Harding (ml); P12: Bobak Ha'Eri (mr); P13: Greg Hume (ml);
P13: 0r14nd0 (b); P15: C.C.A. Christensen (tr), (mr); P16: Sean Kennelly (br); P17: Oscar
Halling (tl); P17: Gustave Dore (mr); P17: Harry Clarke (bl); P21: Wendy Keveney (ml); P25:
Alkivar (ml); P26: David Shankbone (br); P27: Kilnburn (tr); P27: Lee Paxton (b); P28: Ad
Meskens (ml); P30: Cd637 (ml); P30: The White Pelican (ml); P31: Kris Mast (m); P31: J.
Robert Iko (b); P33: Lear 21 (bl); P37: Jan Kronsell (ml); P37: Thomas R Machnitzki (mr);
P37: H. Michael Miley (bl); P41: Quadzilla99adzilla99 (tl); P41: marine 69-71 (ml); P41: steve
lipofsky (mr), (mr); P41: jimcchou (br); P43: transplanted mountaineer (ml)

Series Editor:
Sean Kennelly

Written by
Sean Kennelly
&
Dan Carpenter

Copyright © 2012 Flowerpot Press
a Division of Kamalu LLC, Franklin, TN, U.S.A.
and Mitso Media, Inc., Oakville, ON, Canada

Made in China/Fabriqué en Chine

CONTENTS

GREAT AMERICANS
AMAZING STORIES OF A NATION'S PIONEERS

CONTENTS

GEORGE WASHINGTON
(1732-1799)
FATHER OF HIS COUNTRY

For eight long years during the American Revolution, George Washington was the commanding general of the Colonial army. When the war finally ended in 1783, he just wanted to get back to farming on his lovely Mt. Vernon estate. He wouldn't get to stay long. Six years after the war ended, Washington reluctantly agreed to become the nation's first president. No one ran against him in that election because the nation understood that Washington was the right man for the job. After serving his first four years, he had to be talked into serving a second term. When aides suggested he serve a third term, he flatly refused. Even so, Washington was a superb president because he was a great man. He created a tradition that American presidents must be strong, admirable leaders who could be followed by the people.

George Washington was known as a man who said very little. For example, as president of the four-month long Constitutional Convention in 1787, he only spoke one time during floor debate. He did, however, write a lot of letters. In fact, 19,000 of them still exist. People realized that Washington was a history maker, so they held on to things he wrote. Sadly, his wife, Martha, burned all but three of the letters she and George wrote to each other. She did this to protect their privacy. Though he said little, he certainly looked like a president. Standing 6 feet and 2 inches tall, he towered above most other men. A man who knew Washington said that if 10,000 people were in a room, you would pick Washington as the president.

When his time as president ended in 1797, Washington returned home to tend to the farming he loved so much. Sadly, he would not do so for long. On a cold winter day in 1799, he got caught in the rain while checking his crops. Feeling sick, he came home and went to bed with a sore throat. Modern medicines make such illnesses harmless, but in the 1700s things were different.

Washington died just two days later. He was only 67 years old.

AMAZING TRUTH!

Hippo Teeth?

By the time he became president, Washington only had one tooth left. However, he wore state-of-the-art, hippopotamus tusk teeth, made especially for him with room for his one tooth to fit through.

THOMAS JEFFERSON
(1743-1826)
THE GREAT STATESMAN

Jefferson lived a fascinating life. He was governor of Virginia during the American Revolution, he was the third president, and he founded one of the nation's finest schools, the University of Virginia. But for Jefferson, perhaps his proudest moment was when, at age 33, he wrote the Declaration of Independence. This was a hand-written letter to the British king, informing him the Thirteen Colonies would no longer accept him as their leader. The declaration is powerfully written, and its eloquent words will echo through time... "We hold these truths to be self-evident, that all men are created equal, that they are endowed by their Creator with certain unalienable rights, that among these are life, liberty and the pursuit of happiness…"

Jefferson loved to learn, and he loved to read books. He once said, "I cannot live without books." His personal collection of books was the biggest in America. When he died, those books became the beginning of the Library of Congress, which today has 29 million books and is the largest library in the world. Jefferson's love of learning continued through his excitement over the Louisiana Purchase. He especially delighted in all the information and samples the explorers brought back from the new land.

His love for learning also included training future military leaders. On George Washington's advice, Jefferson convinced Congress to fund the Academy at West Point in New York in 1802. Later, Jefferson continued his quest to educate Americans when he founded the University of Virginia in 1819. The university was located near

his home in Monticello, where he entertained students and professors alike until his death in 1826.

AMAZING TRUTH!

What Are The Odds?

Thomas Jefferson died on July 4, 1826, which was exactly 50 years after the signing of the Declaration of Independence. Amazingly, John Adams, the second president, died on that day as well. Adams's last words were: "Thomas Jefferson survives," but he was wrong; Jefferson had died just a few hours earlier.

MERIWETHER LEWIS & WILLIAM CLARK
(1774-1809) • (1770-1838)

LEWIS

BROTHERS IN ADVENTURE

When Meriwether Lewis was only 5 years old, his father died, and Thomas Jefferson took Lewis under his wing. He praised the boy for his "enterprise, boldness and discretion." He saw in him a great sense of curiosity and adventure. Once he grew, Lewis joined the army on the frontier. There he learned Native American languages and customs. He also met William Clark.

Clark came from a military family. His older brother, General George Rogers Clark, was a Revolutionary War hero. His family moved from Virginia to the Kentucky frontier where he fought against Native American tribes who were attacking settlers. Together, they fought side-by-side.

CLARK

A few years later, Lewis was asked by President Thomas Jefferson to lead a group of explorers across the country to the Pacific Ocean. Jefferson wanted Lewis and his men to map the areas and bring back reports of the land, plants, animals, and the Native American tribes living there. Lewis knew he needed help leading the expedition and asked his old friend, Clark, to join him. Clark was very excited about the expedition!

Together, with about 40 people (mostly hunters and soldiers called the "Corps of Discovery"), Lewis and Clark left St. Louis, Missouri, in May of 1804. They traveled thousands of miles across uncharted rivers, mountains, and prairies. Luckily, they had the help of a French-Canadian fur trader, Toussaint Charbonneau, and his teenage wife, Sacagawea. Sacagawea and her husband knew the territory well and led the men over the Rocky Mountains and down the Clearwater, Snake, and Columbia Rivers. Finally, after 18 long months of exploring and mapping, they reached the Pacific Ocean. They stopped near the present-day city of Portland, Oregon, in November of 1805.

When they finally returned to St. Louis in September of 1806, they shared stories of the vast herds of buffalo and elk. They told of the rivers filled with beavers and the Native American tribes they encountered along the way. Most importantly, their maps became the first maps of the new territory. It showed future settlers and pioneers the way and inspired others to explore the vast land of America.

AMAZING TRUTH!

True Colors

William Clark was called "Red Hair" by Native Americans. They had never seen a red-headed person before.

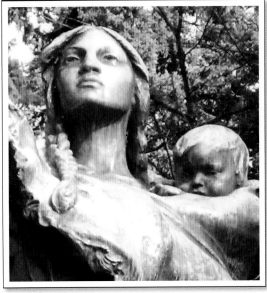

Sacagawea
(1788-1812)
Guiding Light in the Wilderness

It is believed that Native American interpreter, Sacagawea, was born around 1788. It is said she was the daughter of a Shoshone Indian chief, but she only lived among the Shoshone as a child. When she was 12, an enemy tribe, the Hidatsa Indians, raided her camp, and she was taken captive. She was then sold to the trapper, Toussaint Charbonneau, along with another girl known as "Otter Woman." The two became his "wives" and lived with him among the Hidatsa and Mandan Indians near what is now Bismarck, North Dakota, for four years.

Sacagawea was 16 and pregnant with her first child when the Corps of Discovery, led by Lewis and Clark, arrived in the area. Lewis and Clark built a fort there where they spent the winter of 1804-1805 and lived among the Mandan Indians. Charbonneau was hired as a Mandan interpreter for the expedition, but Lewis and Clark soon found that Sacagawea spoke the language better than her husband. So Sacagawea was asked to accompany her husband on the expedition. That winter, Sacagawea gave birth to her son, Jean-Baptiste (who Clark nick-named "Pompey" or "Pomp" for short).

That spring, Sacagawea (along with her husband) led the expedition through the western territories to the Pacific Ocean. Along the way, she acted as the primary interpreter and prevented attack on the expedition. How did she do this? Just by being there. Indian tribes knew that no one would bring a woman and child on a war party, so the expedition was viewed as a peaceful group.

After the expedition, Clark offered to pay for Sacagawea and her husband to relocate to St. Louis. He even offered to pay for Jean-Baptiste's education, but Charbonneau refused and they returned to North Dakota. There, Sacagawea gave birth to a girl, Lisette, and later died at the age of 24. Knowing how fond Clark was of the children, Charbonneau gave them to Clark, and he raised them as his own. Their mother would be forever remembered for the role she played in the history of the United States.

 AMAZING TRUTH!

How Do You Spell That?
Sacagawea? Tsakakawias? Or Sacajawea? The spelling and meaning of Sacagawea's name has varied for years depending on who you ask. Her husband said her name meant "Bird Woman" which in the Hidatsa language would be spelled "Tsakaka-wias." Many spell it with a "j" ("Sacajawea") which is a Shoshone word "Boat-Launcher." Yet in Lewis & Clark's journals, it is mentioned 17 times and spelled with a "g," so for most, it is Sacagawea.

ANDREW JACKSON
(1767-1845)
OLD HICKORY

Andrew Jackson was born in 1767 on the border of North and South Carolina. When Andrew was 14, during the Revolutionary War, the British captured him and his 16-year-old brother, Robert. A Redcoat officer struck each boy on the head with his sword. Andrew was left with a scar for life, but the blow killed his brother. A few months later, Andrew's mother died.

Left alone with no family, young Andrew grew tough as he struggled to survive. In 1788, when he was 21, he moved to the wild Frontier town of Nashville, Tennessee. Nashville was an 8-year-old city where death by Indian attack was a real part of everyday life. Here Jackson became a successful businessman and lawyer, and he entered state politics.

Andrew Jackson became a household name in America in 1815 when he won the Battle of New Orleans. This was the final battle of the War of 1812, and it was one of the most lopsided wins in history. 2,042 British soldiers were killed or wounded, while only 52 American lives were lost. This smashing victory vaulted Jackson into national prominence, leading to his election as president 14 years later.

Jackson was a very important president, because he put politics into the hands of the average American. The six presidents before Jackson were aristocrats, men who tended to be from wealthy families and college educated. Jackson was the first president from the frontier. He was a self-made man of the people. His tough background was evidenced by the fact that he carried two bullets inside him from gun battles. Jackson changed the nature of American politics, making it possible for everyone, regardless of wealth or family status, to play a role in the nation's government.

AMAZING TRUTH!

The Stolen Election
In 1824, Andrew Jackson ran for president for the first time, beating John Quincy Adams by 38,000 votes. He also had more electoral votes than Adams, beating him 99 to 84. However, the Constitution requires a candidate to have more than 50% of the electoral votes to win. So the House of Representatives awarded the presidency to Adams, son of the second president. Jackson was so angry that he began campaigning immediately for the next election, which he won.

ABRAHAM LINCOLN
(1809-1865)
THE GREAT EMANCIPATOR

Abraham Lincoln was born in a log cabin in Kentucky in 1809. Luckily, he was born to a mother who knew how to read and taught young Abe from the time he was a small boy. She also taught him to be honest and good to people. He was also tall. He grew to be six feet and four inches tall! This was one young man everyone had to look up to.

As he grew to manhood, Lincoln continued to borrow and read books. He eventually taught himself enough (by reading law books) to become a lawyer. He also decided to run for political office. Though he lost many times, he never gave up and eventually served in the state legislature and the U.S. Congress. Later, he became president of the United States even though he wasn't on the ballot of 10 southern states.

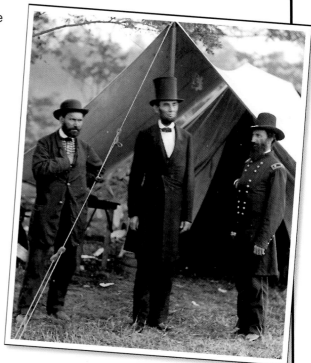

Almost as soon as he took office, the Civil War broke out. It pained Lincoln to see his countrymen at war with each other. In his Gettysburg Address (given after the famous battle), he spoke not only of the ongoing war, but of his hope "that this nation, under God, shall have a new birth of freedom—and that government of the people, by the people, for the people, shall not perish from the earth."

Lincoln also issued the Emancipation Proclamation, finally bringing an end to slavery. Others were not happy with his decisions or the course of the war. Six days after the South surrendered, Lincoln was assassinated by John Wilkes Booth. The nation mourned, but Lincoln's words, works, and memory never left them.

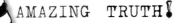

AMAZING TRUTH!

Really Old Cabin
The actual cabin Lincoln was born in is gone, but a similar cabin from the same time period stands on his birthplace near Hodgenville, Kentucky. The 200-year-old cabin is preserved inside a beautiful marble building for all to see. However, the natural spring Lincoln's family drank from is still there, not far from the old cabin.

FREDERICK DOUGLASS
(1818-1895)
VOICE OF THE SLAVES

Frederick Douglass was born into slavery in Maryland in 1818. When he was 12, his owner's wife taught him to read. This was highly unusual, because most slave owners did not want their slaves to read. Slave owners feared that reading would open slaves up to ideas about freedom.

Douglass worked for various owners, but at age 18, he was rented out to a cruel master who whipped him nearly every day. Because of this brutal treatment, Douglass promised himself that he would escape within the year. He tried and failed twice, but the failures to escape only increased his desire to be free. By the time he made his third attempt, he had fallen in love with a free black woman named Anna Murray. She provided him with a sailor's uniform, and by wearing it, he successfully escaped. Now a free man, he wasted no time marrying Anna 12 days later. The two settled in Massachusetts and had five children during their 44 years of marriage.

Three years after escaping, Douglass was asked to speak at an abolitionist meeting about his experiences as a slave. His speech was very powerful, and painted a true, but horrible, picture of slavery. He now began to speak regularly, and because he was such a gifted speaker, large audiences would always gather to hear him. His speeches were very important because they helped inform northerners of the terrors of slavery. This fed a growing northern anger over the use of slaves in the South, which eventually helped abolish slavery in America.

The issue of slavery divided Americans in the mid-1800s. Violent episodes such as Bleeding Kansas and John Brown's raid on Harper's Ferry forced Americans to take sides. Eventually, a four-year-long war (the Civil War) was fought to settle the issue. When the war was over, the practice of slavery was ended forever in America. Americans have Frederick Douglass to thank for helping make that a reality.

AMAZING TRUTH!

The Voice of Reason
Douglass was such an eloquent speaker that many people doubted he could have ever been enslaved. In order to prove he had indeed once been a slave, Douglass wrote his autobiography, *The Life and Times of Frederick Douglass*, in 1845. The terrors of slavery depicted in the book helped many Americans understand that a civilized nation could no longer allow slavery to take place within its boundaries.

Harriet Tubman
(1820-1913)
Freedom Fighter

Harriet Tubman was born Araminta "Minty" Ross to slave parents. As a child, she was taught to resist slave owners by her mother, Harriet. Her mother worked hard to keep their family together. When her owner came with a buyer for Tubman's younger brother, Tubman's mother threatened the owner and his buyer saying, "You are after my son; but the first man that comes into my house, I will split his head open." The bold move inspired Tubman who escaped years later in 1849 in the middle of the night. Upon reaching the free state of Pennsylvania, Tubman wrote, "I looked at my hands to see if I was the same person now (that) I was free. There was such a glory over everything…and I felt like I was in Heaven."

Tubman took the name of Harriet, honoring the mother who inspired her daring escape. Her last name came from the free man she married, John Tubman. Though he was free, he was unwilling to help her escape, and she never returned to him. Tubman made a number of bold trips into slave territory to rescue the rest of her family and other slaves. She often made her trips during the winter when people would be indoors and less likely to notice runaway slaves. She worked with other abolitionists, including Frederick Douglass, using the famous Underground Railroad – a series of safe homes and hiding places that helped the slaves to safely escape to the North. Of Tubman, Douglass said, "The midnight sky and the silent stars have been the witnesses of your devotion to freedom and of your heroism."

Tubman went on to serve as a nurse and a spy during the Civil War, knowing a victory by the North would result in freedom for the slaves. She even led an armed group of Union soldiers in a raid on some plantations in South Carolina that freed 700 slaves. When the war ended and all the slaves were freed, she continued to fight for equality. She also lent her voice to women's rights, working alongside Susan B. Anthony before Tubman's death in 1913. Her story continues to inspire people fighting for equality and civil rights.

HARRIET TUBMAN.

AMAZING TRUTH!

When's Your Birthday?

Since she was born into slavery, the true age of Harriett Tubman was never known. Most slave owners rarely kept birth records. Her death certificate lists her year of birth as 1815 while her gravestone is carved with the year 1820. Tubman herself had no real idea since she listed her birth year as 1820 on some documents and 1822 or 1825 on others.

ROBERT E. LEE
(1807-1870)
THE TACTICIAN

Robert E. Lee was born in Virginia in 1807 to a famous Revolutionary War general, "Light Horse Harry" Lee. Young Lee attended the U.S. Military Academy at West Point, and then served for 32 years in the U.S. Army.

When the Civil War began, Lee was the most respected officer in the army, so Lincoln offered Lee the top command position for the war. Lee declined the offer and then resigned from the army, saying he must remain true to his home state of Virginia. Confederate president, Jefferson Davis, quickly commissioned Lee into the Confederate Army, where he became its leading commander.

Robert E. Lee was probably the greatest American battle commander who ever lived. During the Civil War, Lee won battle after battle, though he was nearly always under-supplied and outnumbered. An example of this was at the Battle of Chancellorsville, where Lee found his Rebel army of 56,000 men facing a massive Union army of 135,000 men. Amazingly, Lee not only won this battle, but he ran the Union army off the battlefield, forcing them to flee across the Rappahannock River under the cover of darkness.

Lee was famous for dividing his army into two groups, even when heavily outnumbered. At the second Battle of Bull Run, he sent half of his army all the way around to the rear of the Union forces. This caused the Union general to lose track of both parts of Lee's army, and, of course, it led to yet another Southern

victory. Lee divided his army in a similar way in the Seven Days Battle. This so confused the Northern general that he reported Lee was using 200,000 troops, when he, in fact, had only 85,000.

Only late in the war, when Northern advantages in numbers and supplies took their toll, did Lee find it impossible to continue to outwit Union generals. When the war finally ended, Lee's once proud Army of Northern Virginia was starving and out of ammunition, a shadow of its former self.

AMAZING TRUTH!

Stolen Mansion
Robert E. Lee lived in Arlington, Virginia, in the Custis-Lee Mansion, a home built by George Washington's adopted grandson. Just a month after the Civil War began, the Union army turned the mansion's yard into a cemetery, placing graves all the way up to the front porch. This was to make sure Lee could never return and occupy the beautiful home. Those graves became the beginning of Arlington National Cemetery, the nation's primary military graveyard.

ULYSSES S. GRANT
(1822-1885)
THE HERO OF APPOMATTOX

When Ulysses S. Grant was born in Ohio in 1822, his parents named him Hiram Ulysses Grant. But he never liked the fact that his initials spelled "HUG," and as he left home at 18 to attend the United States Military Academy, he hoped to change his name. Oddly, he got the chance the moment he arrived on campus. The congressman who recommended him to the school had errantly written Grant's name down as Ulysses S. Grant. When Grant saw the new name, he liked the change. For the rest of his life, his only middle name was "S."

During the first three years of the Civil War, President Lincoln could not find a general who understood how to take the large and powerful Union Army into Virginia and win the war. During that period, Lincoln's

Army of the Potomac lost battle after battle, as he went through eight commanding generals. Finally, in 1863, Lincoln realized the best general in his army was Ulysses S. Grant. Grant had won a series of amazing victories in Mississippi and Tennessee.

Grant was brought to Washington and put in charge of the Army of the Potomac. Lincoln ordered him to defeat Robert E. Lee and win the war. Grant plotted a straight line from D.C. to the Rebel capitol of Richmond, just 90 miles south. Beginning in the spring of 1864, Grant and Lee fought a brutal series of battles that filled up Northern hospitals and produced over 100,000 Union casualties. However, when the smoke cleared in April 1864, Grant had overpowered and outlasted Lee. The two met in a house at a town called Appomattox Court House, Virginia. Here Lee surrendered his army to Grant, ending the worst loss of life in American history. Grant was the man who ended the war.

AMAZING TRUTH!

A General's Love

Grant was well-known for his love of cigars. He smoked up to 20 cigars a day. When the war ended, a grateful nation mailed him stogies by the barrelful to thank him for his service to the country.

"BUFFALO BILL" CODY
(1846-1917)
SHOWMAN OF THE WEST

William F. Cody, or "Buffalo Bill," was born on the frontier of Iowa to Canadian parents who opposed slavery. Cody's father was stabbed by a member of a proslavery mob and eventually died. At the age of 11, Cody went to work as a mounted messenger and a scout. He soon became very skilled at horse wrangling, fighting Indians, and hunting.

He joined the army during the Civil War at the age of 17. After the war, he worked again as a civilian scout (someone who is not a soldier) for the U.S. Army in Kansas. Then he took a job as a buffalo hunter for the Union Pacific Railroad to provide food for the construction crews. He killed over 4,000 buffalo in a two-year period and was given the nickname, "Buffalo Bill."

He was soon in demand as an expert scout and marksman. He knew Indian ways and displayed great courage and endurance. The U.S. Army often used him to help wipe out any Native Americans who opposed white settlement. He was even awarded the Medal of Honor in 1872.

His adventures were soon known by the world through newspapers and books. The books described him as a hard-riding, fast-shooting, western folk hero. Cody was offered a part in a dramatized play about the Wild West (called "*The Scout of the Prairie*") with other famous western people like "Wild Bill" Hickok.

After 10 years of doing the show, Cody created his own show, "*Buffalo Bill's Wild West Show*," in 1883 that toured all over the U.S. and Europe, including a show for Queen Victoria in England. The show featured the famous markswoman Annie Oakley, and the legendary Chief Sitting Bull with 20 of his braves. The show gave crowds a "safe" taste of the West and made Cody one of the most well-known celebrities in the world. At his death in 1917, tributes were made by King Edward of England, Kaiser Wilhelm of Germany, and President Woodrow Wilson, to name a few.

AMAZING TRUTH!

If You Build It, They Will Come
The town of Cody, WY, and the east entrance to Yellowstone National Park are part of the legacy of "Buffalo Bill" Cody. He scouted the area and lobbied the federal government to allow the new entrance. He even paid for the construction of the east entrance out of his own pocket. He also helped create the town of Cody, launched its first newspaper, built hotels, and got the railroad to come. That's a legend in action!

BRIGHAM YOUNG
(1801-1877)
COLONIZER OF THE WEST

Born in Vermont in 1801, Brigham Young was apprenticed as a carpenter and a glazier (glass worker) at the age of 14. Years later, he became a follower of the Mormon prophet, Joseph Smith. When Smith was killed by an armed mob in 1844, Young was soon established as the new leader of the church. In this role, he had a major influence in the settlement of the West.

Under Young's leadership, thousands of Mormons (members of the Church of Jesus Christ of Latter-day Saints) headed west on a modern exodus to the "promised land" of Utah where they could live in peace. They even blazed a path on the opposite side of the river from the Oregon Trail to avoid any further trouble. When they first arrived in the Salt Lake Valley, Young declared, "This is the right place." Yet "Brother Brigham" didn't stop there. He sent settlers to colonize the rest of Utah and areas of Idaho, Wyoming, Nevada, Arizona, California, southern Colorado and northern Mexico. Some of these settlements we know today as San Bernardino, CA, Las Vegas, NV, and Mesa, AZ.

Young was the first governor of the Utah Territory, which included Nevada, western Colorado, and part of Wyoming. He led the people (Mormon and non-Mormon) to lay the foundations of modern civilization in the west including roads and bridges, forts, irrigation projects, government (he organized the first legislature and the first postal service), the arts (he directed the creation of the Mormon Tabernacle Choir), and education. In fact, he started rival schools, first organizing the University of Deseret (now known as the University of Utah) and later creating Brigham Young Academy, which became Brigham Young University.

AMAZING TRUTH!

Adobe, Sandstone or Granite? Brigham Young once considered constructing the great Mormon temple in Salt Lake City out of adobe. Then he chose sandstone, but it cracked. Finally, he decided on solid granite. The only problem? It could take an entire day to transport one block of granite from the quarry 20 miles away. So they constructed a railroad which allowed them to get dozens of stones to the site every day.

MARK TWAIN
(1835-1910)
THE FATHER OF AMERICAN LITERATURE

Storytelling was always in Samuel Clemens' blood. While his father was an unsmiling, strict man, his mother would often spin entertaining tales for the children. Perhaps she's the reason why Clemens (later known as "Mark Twain") would one day be called "The Father of American Literature" by several major authors including Ernest Hemmingway, William Faulkner, and playwright, Eugene O'Neil?

Growing up in the river port of Hannibal, Missouri, in the mid-1800s forever influenced Twain's life and writings. However, poverty also influenced much of Twain's early life due to his father's death in 1847. Many of his choices were an attempt to find riches and respect as well as adventure. He became a riverboat captain at age 21 – a very prestigious and well-paid job, similar to a commercial jet pilot today. Unfortunately, he was forced to quit when the Civil War broke out. Twain then left Missouri to prospect for gold in Nevada and California. He never found the gold but found a job writing for a newspaper. He had written for his brother, Orion, in Hannibal and soon took to writing like a fish takes to water. It was then he decided to call himself Mark Twain – a riverboat term for 12 feet of water.

Riverboats, and the wide variety of characters they attracted, soon filled his writing. Some of his characters hinted at social problems – like the murderous Injun Joe, a tough-drinking Native American, and Jim, an escaped slave. More than anything, though, his books painted an adventurous picture of what life was like for young boys like Tom Sawyer or Huck Finn who lived on the mighty Mississippi River. His common-man attitude, humor and wit were felt on every page. And his truthful take on American life became a national treasure.

D'où viens-tu? me demanda l'un d'eux.

AMAZING TRUTH!

A Deathly Prophecy

Twain was born in 1835, when Haley's Comet was in the sky, and he predicted he would die when the comet returned. He was right, he passed away upon the comet's return in 1910.

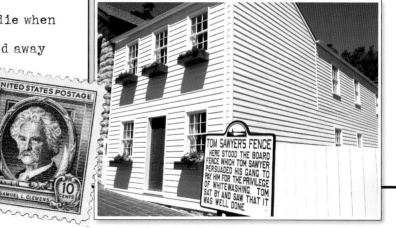

Edgar Allan Poe
(1809-1849)
American Gothic

Edgar Allan Poe was born to a family of actors in 1809. Death entered the picture early when his mother died when he was only two years old. He was taken to a childless friend, John Allan, whose wife raised him as her own. Poe was sent to England and Scotland for his early school years. He then went to study at the University of Virginia, but he gambled away his money. He moved to Boston, Massachusetts, where he began writing and publishing poetry.

Like many poets, he made no money in the effort. He soon became so poor he joined the military using a false name. When Allan, his foster father, found out, he paid money to have him released and got him into the U.S. Military Academy at West Point. But Poe had no patience for the military. His writing called to him.

Poe moved to Baltimore, Maryland, and published more poetry. He began taking a string of jobs as a newspaper writer and editor. He continued to publish more poetry and some stories such as *The Fall of the House of Usher*. He also is credited with starting the detective genre with his story, *The Murders of the Rue Morgue*. A short time later he wrote his most famous poem, "The Raven." It told the tale of a sad and mournful man who wishes he could bring back his beloved Lenore. The poem represented the sadness Poe often felt in his life. "The Raven" was a big hit and made Poe a very famous writer.

Though he was a literary artist, he did not depend on artistic impulses alone to write his stories or poems. He treated his writing as work, outlining and planning his writing. In fact, French poets Charles Baudelaire and Stéphane Mallarmé praised his methods, calling him a master poet and writer. Most of all, he is known for his dark imagination and the beauty of his haunting stories of horror. Perhaps he spent too much time thinking about death and other mysteries. He was found dead on the streets of Baltimore, Maryland, just after his 40th birthday wearing clothes that were not his own. No one knows for sure why he died, but his words will be with us evermore.

AMAZING TRUTH!

The Parrot?

Poe once considered using a parrot as the bird in his famous poem, "The Raven." But a colorful parrot did not fit the sad tone of his poem, so he chose a raven since it was a symbol of superstition and bad omens. Raven want a cracker?!

Geronimo
(1829-1909)
The Last Apache

In 1829, Geronimo was born into the Apache Indian tribe, a group of Native Americans who lived in Texas, New Mexico, Arizona, and northern Mexico. As Mexican and American settlers moved into the area during the 1800s, they found the Apache to be unwilling to let go of the land. Regular fighting took place as a result, and because Geronimo was a young warrior, he was part of the violence. But in 1858, his life changed forever when Mexican soldiers killed his wife and their three children. This fueled a hatred for settlers that Geronimo held onto for the rest of his life.

A half-century of warfare led to the gradual reduction of the Apache tribe, and by 1876, the U.S. government

ordered that all Apache must move to the dismal San Carlos Reservation in southern Arizona. Like many proud Indian warriors, Geronimo had no interest in reservation life, and he and many other Apache held out as the U.S. Army attempted to round up his people.

Though Geronimo was not a chief, Native Americans viewed him as a leader due to his courage in battle. White settlers knew Geronimo well, calling him "the worst Indian who ever lived." Because he was so feared, the U.S. government sent 5,000 troops to track him down and capture him, dead or alive.

Finally, in 1886, Geronimo found himself hopelessly surrounded and outnumbered, and he realized he could fight no more. A negotiator told him that if he surrendered he would be sent to Florida for a short time, and then would be allowed to return to his home in Arizona. However, once captured, he remained a prisoner for the rest of his days. He was held in camps in Florida and Oklahoma, and was never allowed to return to Arizona.

For the American public, fear of Geronimo turned to fascination. Geronimo sold souvenirs of himself, appeared in fairs, and even rode in Teddy Roosevelt's 1905 inaugural parade. But sadly, in February 1909, he was thrown from his horse and laid on the cold ground all night until a friend found him. Pneumonia set in, and he died just days later. Before dying, he confided that he regretted ever allowing soldiers to take him alive.

AMAZING TRUTH!

Grave Robbers!
It is rumored that some Yale University students visited his gravesite in Oklahoma and stole Geronimo's skull during World War I. The rumor holds that the students dug up Geronimo in 1918 and brought his skull and silver bridle back to a secret location on their campus. In 1986, a lawyer representing students at Yale denied that the skull was on the campus. Even so, in 2009, descendants of Geronimo sued to get his skull back, but they had no success in their effort.

CRAZY HORSE
(1840-1877)
THE GREAT SIOUX

Crazy Horse was a chief of the Sioux Indians, a massive group of tribes that dominated the northern Great Plains. The California gold rush of 1849 and the Colorado gold rush of 1859 brought white settlers into Sioux territory, and this led to frequent gun battles between U.S. soldiers and Sioux warriors. During this time, Crazy Horse became well-known due to his leadership role in the 1866 Fetterman Massacre. This was an episode in which

Crazy Horse tricked 81 U.S. soldiers into leaving the safety of their fort to chase after a small band of Indians. Crazy Horse led 2,000 Arapaho, Cheyenne, and Sioux warriors in an ambush of the U.S. soldiers, killing them all.

Conflict between the Sioux nation and the U.S. government seemed to be resolved in 1868, when the Treaty of Fort Laramie gave the Sioux a massive reservation in and around current day South Dakota. However, gold was discovered on the reservation in an area called the Black Hills in 1874, so the U.S. government offered the Sioux $6 million for the land that had gold. The Sioux refused, so U.S. troops forced the Indians off the land. This led to the battle of the Little Big Horn, one of the most amazing battles in U.S. history. Here, Crazy Horse and fellow Sioux Chief, Sitting Bull, killed over 260 U.S. soldiers, including their leader, George Custer. Even so, the Sioux eventually lost the war and had to give up their rights to the Black Hills.

In 1877, just one year after his magnificent victory at the Little Big Horn, Crazy Horse turned himself in to U.S. authorities. He agreed to live peacefully on a reservation. However, four months after moving onto the reservation, U.S. authorities attempted to place Crazy Horse under arrest. A scuffle took place, and a soldier used a bayonet to stab the Indian chief. Crazy Horse died that night.

AMAZING TRUTH!

World's Largest Statue
A statue of Crazy Horse, that could one day be among the largest stone statues in the world, is currently being carved into the Black Hills of South Dakota. Carving began in 1948 on the Crazy Horse Monument, and in 1998 the head of Crazy Horse was completed. That portion alone is 87-feet tall, which is much taller than the heads of the U.S. presidents at nearby Mt. Rushmore.

BENJAMIN FRANKLIN
(1706-1790)
AMERICA'S FOUNDING FATHER

From the time he was a small boy, Benjamin Franklin was coming up with inventions and ideas. He was constantly on the lookout for ways to improve just about everything in life. He even created swim fins as a boy so he could swim faster.

He started out his working career as a printing apprentice, and before long, he was writing and editing a successful newspaper. He also printed his famous book of wit and wisdom, *Poor Richard's Almanack*. This book made Franklin a wealthy man, and he soon dived into even more pursuits. He helped start the University of Pennsylvania. He conducted science experiments with electricity and invented the lightning rod to protect homes from lightning strikes. He also invented things like bi-focals to help people (himself included) see better in their old age. Franklin was the first postmaster and started the first lending library in America, as well as the first fire department in Pennsylvania.

Best of all, Franklin was known as a diplomat and a courageous statesman. He opposed injustice wherever it occurred and even got England to repeal the hated Stamp Act that unfairly taxed the American colonies. He often represented America in foreign nations like France and Sweden. Of course, he was instrumental in the creation of the Declaration of Independence along with Thomas Jefferson, John Adams, Roger Sherman and Robert Livingston. During the Revolutionary War, he was also able to convince France to help America. In fact, it was the French ships that helped win the important battle at Yorktown. When the U.S. Constitution was created after the war, Franklin was there to add his voice of wisdom and reason. To this day, Franklin's name and face can be found in cities, counties, companies, navy ships, and even on U.S. stamps and currency.

AMAZING TRUTH!

Don't Try This At Home!
Benjamin Franklin once flew a kite in a thunderstorm to prove that lightning had an electrical charge. He made sure he was grounded so he wouldn't be electrocuted. Other people tried to duplicate his experiment and didn't understand the need to be grounded. They got quite a shock. Ouch!

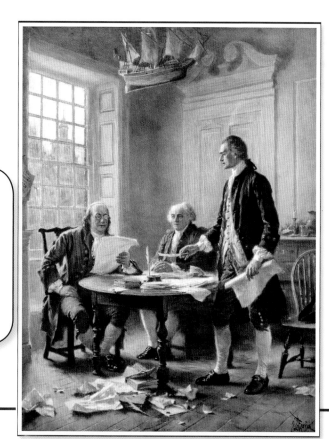

THOMAS EDISON
(1847-1931)
THE WIZARD

Thomas Edison was born in 1847 in Milan, Ohio, and started experiments in science and business at an early age. He actually burned down his father's barn in one failed attempt, but Edison never saw his experiments as failures. He once said in his later years, "I have not failed. I've just found 10,000 ways that won't work!" As a boy, he sold candy and newspapers on trains in Michigan as well as selling vegetables on the side. He developed a keen business sense in those early years that would serve him well as an adult.

His next job came when he saved the station agent's 3-year-old son from a runaway train. The station agent was so grateful that he trained Edison as a telegraph operator. The job didn't last long, though. Edison asked for a night shift so he could devote time to his two favorite activities – reading and experimenting. Unfortunately, he spilled sulfuric acid during an experiment one night. The acid leaked down through the floorboards and onto his boss' desk. He was fired the next day, but within two years he had gotten his first patent. It was for an electric vote recorder, and it would be the first of over a thousand patents.

In Menlo Park, New Jersey (now renamed Edison, NJ), Edison developed what would be known as the first industrial research lab. Edison knew he needed help to get past the failures and find the solutions, so he employed many others to work with him in the lab. There they created a host of inventions, many of which bear his name. Up until his death in 1931, he was constantly pushing the boundaries of technology and innovation.

Most people are aware of his invention of the first practical electric light bulb and the fact that he started General Electric (or GE, as it's known today). His accomplishments seemed so magical to the public that they called him the "Wizard of Menlo Park." A few of his other creations (and that of his lab) were the phonograph (the first device to allow you to record and playback music or voice), power systems (to power his new light bulb), and the first movie camera (the kinetograph) and movie viewer (the kinetoscope).
He truly was a wiz!

I want to see a Phonograph in every American Home
Thomas A. Edison

The New Edison
Thomas A. Edison's
Final Achievement

AMAZING TRUTH!

Edison's Amazing Warehouse
Edison wanted his lab to have anything an inventor would need to experiment. So he stocked it with everything imaginable: 8,000 kinds of chemicals, every kind of screw made, every size of needle, every kind of cord or wire, human and animal hair, silk, cocoons, animal hoofs, shark's teeth, deer horns, tortoise shell, cork, resin, varnish and oil, ostrich feathers, a peacock's tail, amber, rubber, all ores, and even more!

HELEN KELLER
(1880-1968)
A VOICE OUT OF THE DARKNESS

Helen Keller was an unusually bright child. She was walking and talking by her first birthday. Six months later, she fell ill to an unknown disease and became deaf and blind. As she grew older, though, her frustration with her condition pushed her parents to find a teacher to help young Helen.

Anne Sullivan came to the Keller plantation in Alabama. Once she arrived, she tried to teach Helen sign language for the different objects around her. Helen just got more frustrated, but Sullivan didn't give up. She took Helen to a cottage on the plantation away from the rest of the family. There, Sullivan got Helen to make the connection between the words she was spelling in her hands and the world around her. Sullivan pumped water over Helen's hands as she spelled out W-A-T-E-R in them. Finally, Helen understood and demanded that Sullivan teach her more. That first day she learned 30 new words in sign language, and that was just the beginning.

Helen attended college with Anne Sullivan as an interpreter. With her help, Helen was able to earn a bachelor's degree – the first for a blind/deaf person. After college, she wrote her own autobiography and lectured around the country and the world. She also helped found the American Civil Liberties Union (ACLU) in 1920. Eventually, her story was made into a movie just before her death. It's a story that continues to inspire millions to overcome their own personal obstacles.

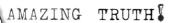

AMAZING TRUTH!

Friends in High Places
Helen Keller's story caught the attention of author Mark Twain. They soon became friends, and he introduced her to millionaire Henry Rogers of Standard Oil. He was so impressed with Helen's determination and drive that he agreed to fund her education. Helen would never forget the act and dedicated one of her books to Rogers and his wife.

Helen Keller, No. 12.

ANDREW CARNEGIE
(1835-1919)
THE ORIGINAL MAN OF STEEL

Andrew Carnegie was born in Scotland in 1835, and his family moved to America when he was 12. They settled near Pittsburgh, Pennsylvania, where Andrew worked 12 hours a day in a factory, dipping machine parts in hot oil. This was a terrible job, but it was typical for many children in the time period. The factory owner knew young Andrew was very smart, so he was moved into the factory office. He was promoted many times and eventually found himself working as an assistant to a powerful railroad company executive.

The executive liked Andrew, and gave him valuable stock tips – advice about how to make money buying and selling stocks. Andrew followed the advice. By the time he was in his mid-twenties, these stock purchases made Andrew a wealthy man. In 1863, when he was just 27, he was making $2,400 a year from his railroad salary, but he made an additional $45,000 from his stock market investments.

Carnegie needed places to invest his money. He looked for business opportunities, and discovered the steel industry. Steel is a much stronger and lighter form of iron, and it was just coming into use in the mid-1800s. There was a huge demand for the metal, because it was ideal for railroad tracks and skyscrapers. So as America expanded into a superpower, steel would be an essential ingredient. The world's steel was mostly made in Britain at the time, so Carnegie saw a chance to get in early on an industry that was about to really take off. Carnegie traveled to Britain to observe their steel mills in action. He returned home and built a massive steel mill on the south side of Pittsburgh.

Like Rockefeller, he knew how to cut costs and undersell his opponents. He also pursued vertical integration, obtaining coalmines to power his plant, iron ore mines, and railroads to haul his product. By the 1880s, he was America's biggest steel producer, and by the 1890s his company alone was making more steel than all of Britain combined. His presence earned Pittsburgh the nickname "Steel City," which is why its professional football team is called the Steelers.

By 1901, Carnegie was ready to get out of the business. He sold his company for $492 million in a deal arranged by the famous banker, J.P. Morgan. Once the deal was made, Morgan told Carnegie, "congratulations on being the world's richest man." Morgan added other steel mills to Carnegie's to create The United States Steel Corporation. It had a market value of $1.4 billion, making it the nation's first billion-dollar company.

AMAZING TRUTH!

Library Love

Carnegie is especially remembered for giving his wealth away. He believed it was a disgrace for a wealthy man to die with all his cash. He gave away over $400 million in his lifetime – over 90 percent of what he made. He especially loved to pay for libraries. There are over 2000 Carnegie libraries in the world today.

CHARLES LINDBERGH
(1902-1974)
PLANE AMAZING

Charles Lindbergh, or "Lucky Lindy" as he was later known, was born in Detroit, Michigan, in 1902, but spent much of his childhood in Minnesota. In fact, his father went on to serve as a U.S. congressman from Minnesota for 10 years. His mother was a school teacher, and he often moved from school to school. Through it all, Lindbergh had a growing interest in motorized engines. First it was cars, but then the invention of airplanes captured his imagination. He actually dropped out of his mechanical engineering program at the University of Wisconsin to enter a flying school in Nebraska.

Within a year, Lindbergh bought his first airplane and toured around the country as a daredevil barnstormer performing aerial stunts. Then he trained as an Army Air Service pilot, graduating at the top of his class despite crashing a plane just eight days before the end of training. It was peacetime though, so Lindbergh found work as an air mail pilot.

Then a French-born hotel owner, Raymond Orteig, offered $25,000 to the first pilot who would make a solo, transatlantic flight from New York to Paris. Many tried and failed (six pilots died in the attempt), but Lindbergh knew it could be done. He got some St. Louis businessmen to support his effort and oversaw the design of the plane. On May 20th, 1927, Lindbergh flew into the great unknown. He fought fog, ice, and fatigue, and finally landed in Paris 33.5 hours later. Life would never be the same for "Lucky Lindy."

Lindbergh was hailed by U.S. and world leaders for his accomplishment. He was awarded the Medal of Honor and the Distinguished Flying Cross. His plane, the *Spirit of St. Louis* was featured on stamps within a month of his feat. He was also asked to consult or advise aviation efforts around the globe. Lindbergh was also a huge supporter of scientist, Robert Goddard, and helped him get the money necessary to develop rocket engines.

Sadly, Lindbergh's baby boy was kidnapped, and he and his wife became very private after the event. In his later years, he continued to advise the U.S. Air Force and even won a Pulitzer Prize in 1954 for his book about his famous flight called, *The Spirit of St. Louis*. Just a few years before his death, he witnessed the launch of *Apollo 11* as they rocketed away to the Moon.

AMAZING TRUTH!

Turn Left Where?

On his famous flight to Paris, Lindbergh used every method known to man to navigate: instruments, the stars, guessing, and asking directions. As Lindbergh flew low over the ocean, he spotted some fishing boats. He tried to circle and ask if they would point the way toward land. But they couldn't hear him and he flew on, finally finding the coast of Ireland on his way to France.

DAGENS NYHETER.

LINDBERGH HÖLL ORD

STEG UR MASKINEN I HALMHATT 10.21 E. M. PÅ LE BOURGET.

Stormande jubel hälsar den djärve vid färdens mål.

SALLY RIDE
(1951-)
SPACEWOMAN

Dr. Sally Kirsten Ride was born in Encino, California, in 1951. From an early age, her parents encouraged her and her sister, Karen, to do their best and study hard in school. Sally showed an early interest in science, so her parents subscribed to *Scientific American* magazine to encourage her to learn more.

Sally also found she had talent for sports, particularly tennis. She was very good and almost became a professional tennis player. She even left college to try to improve her skills. After a few months, though, she decided to return to college. She launched into learning, becoming a doctor in physics (also called a Ph.D.).

As she was finishing her degree, NASA put an advertisement in the student newspaper asking for scientists who were interested in becoming part of the space shuttle missions. Sally applied, and out of 8,000 people, she was one of 35 people selected! Six were women – the first female astronauts ever selected for the U.S. space program!

Sally trained hard for four years doing physical training and flight training as well as studying more science, math, meteorology (weather and climate), guidance, navigation, and everything about the shuttle. Finally, in June of 1983, Sally lifted off as part of the crew of the Space Shuttle *Challenger*. Not only was she the first American woman in space, but, at 32, she was also the youngest astronaut ever! A little over a year later, she flew on another shuttle mission and was scheduled for a third mission when disaster struck. In 1986, the Space Shuttle *Challenger* blew up just after launch. Sally would help NASA discover the reasons why it exploded, but she would never fly another space mission.

Sally knew she wouldn't be an astronaut forever and had already decided to become a teacher. She taught physics at the University of California at San Diego and was the director of the California Space Institute. She also wrote books for elementary and middle school kids to encourage them (especially girls) to study science and reach for the stars, just like she did!

AMAZING TRUTH!

Space or Tennis Ace?
Sally Ride almost became a professional tennis player instead of an astronaut and teacher. She was ranked 18th on the national junior tennis circuit and had a promising future. Even tennis legend Billy Jean King felt she had the talent to be a pro tennis player. Good thing she decided to go back to college, or someone else might have been the first American woman in space!

OPRAH WINFREY
(1954-)
VOICE OF THE COMMON MAN

Oprah Winfrey was born in rural Kosciusko, Mississippi, to a teenage mother. She was so poor she wore dresses made of potato sacks. Her grandmother taught her to read before she was three, and she could recite Bible verses at an early age. She was also known for playing games where she would interview her corncob doll and the crows that would perch on the fence near her home.

Then she moved to an inner-city neighborhood with her mother in Milwaukee, Wisconsin. It was a dark time for Winfrey. She was abused by relatives, but no one believed her. She made some poor choices that almost trapped her in a life of poverty. Finally, she moved to Nashville, TN, to live with her father where she began to find her voice.

In high school, Winfrey won 2nd place in a national speech contest! She started doing the news part-time on a local radio station. After college, she worked as a news anchor (a person who tells the news) on a TV station in Nashville, then Baltimore, Maryland, and finally Chicago, Illinois, where she was the host of AM Chicago. Within a few months, her ratings (how many people watch a TV show) went from last to first place! So they changed the name of the show to The Oprah Winfrey Show and started broadcasting nationally in 1986.

Winfrey's show was the number-one talk show in America from that time until its final show in May of 2011. It appealed to so many people because she was so genuine and likable, often shedding tears when told heartfelt stories by her guests. She enabled them to open up and reveal things they never told any other talk show host. She was able to get interviews no other show could get, like Michael Jackson at the height of his fame in 1993 (the most watched interview in the history of television)! She even got an Academy Award nomination for her role in filmmaker Steven Spielberg's *The Color Purple*. Soon everyone followed Winfrey's every move, and she created a media brand that made her one of the wealthiest people on the planet. Money wasn't her only goal, though. She wanted social change. Her shows often prompted people to read books and consider other points of view, and brought a variety of topics to national attention. Today, Winfrey continues to be an inspiration to America and the world!

AMAZING TRUTH!

Hey Orpah!

Though she is known around the world as Oprah Winfrey, she was actually named after Orpah — a biblical character in the Book of Ruth. So how did she become "Oprah"? Her family and friends couldn't pronounce the unusual name and just called her "Oprah." The name stuck!

WALT DISNEY
(1901-1966)
SUPREME IMAGINEER

From his days as a boy in rural Marceline, Missouri, Walt Disney was a ball of creative energy. From his first brush with art, Disney was hooked. He loved to draw and paint his world. He even painted pictures of farmyard animals on the side of his father's barn… in tar! His father was furious, but his mother saw the budding artist and encouraged him whenever she had the opportunity.

As he grew older, Disney continued to draw. He teamed up with fellow artist, Ub Iwerks, and together they started a company to create animated short films for local businesses. Disney wasn't much of a businessman, and the company failed.

Disney then moved to California and teamed up with his older brother, Roy. Roy provided the financial guidance and business sense Walt lacked. With his brother's support, Walt kept trying. When their Oswald the Lucky Rabbit character was taken from them in a bad business deal, Walt created a new character – Mickey Mouse (with the help of his old friend, Ub Iwerks). The Disney Brothers never looked back. Mickey brought success to the company and paved the way for *Snow White*, the first animated feature film. Despite gloomy predictions, the film was a huge success! Disney was even awarded one large and seven miniature Oscars for the achievement (one for each dwarf)!

Over the years, Disney went on to create a number of animated and live-action films at his ever-growing studio. Then, he took some of his artists and studio craftsman and gave them the task of creating an all-new type of entertainment – Disneyland. He called them imagineers since they used their imagination to engineer a new kind of amusement park for families. Though Disney died 11 years after Disneyland first opened, his legacy is found around the world in theme parks, entertainment, and the hearts of those who dare to dream!

AMAZING TRUTH!

Daddy's Day

Saturdays were "Daddy's Day" when Walt Disney took his daughters to Griffith Park to ride the carousel. While he sat and watched them from a park bench, he wished for a more ideal place where families could share fun together. A few years later, Disneyland was born, and families have enjoyed the magic ever since!

FRANKLIN DELANO ROOSEVELT
(1882-1945)
ARCHITECT OF THE NEW DEAL

Franklin Delano Roosevelt was born in New York in 1882. He was an only child, and his mother showered him with attention – so much so, in fact, that when he went away to Harvard in 1900 she went with him, taking an apartment near his. After college, he entered politics and eventually became the governor of New York in 1929.

In 1921, when he was 39 years old, Roosevelt went for a swim in a lake in Maine while on vacation there. After the swim, he went straight to bed, feeling so tired that he could not even remove his swimsuit. He fell asleep, but later woke with a 104-degree temperature. He had been stricken by Polio. The Polio Virus had attacked his spinal cord, and he would be paralyzed from the waste down for the rest of his life.

For the next eight years he worked as hard as he could to beat the disability. He would fight for hours at a time, covered in sweat, to move one leg in front of the other. But his iron will could not overcome the reality of Polio. He gave up the struggle in 1929, when he became governor of New York. His legs grew feeble, and late in his life they were withered and tiny, although his upper body remained robust.

In 1929, the New York Stock Exchange crashed. Nearly overnight, billions of dollars in stocks simply disappeared, one third of working Americans lost their jobs, and America plunged into the Great Depression. With the nation's economy in terrible trouble, Roosevelt was elected president in 1932.

Roosevelt felt that the government needed to actively work to create jobs and "prime the pump" of the economy to get it started again. He called his program the New Deal, and he created thousands of jobs in his effort to get Americans back to work. These newly created government programs put men to work building dams, roads, post offices, and schools. Swamps were drained, trees were planted, and even artists were paid to create art that depicted the events of the era.

Roosevelt was re-elected in 1936, and then, in 1940, something that had never happened took place; the president was elected for a third term. Tradition held that presidents only serve two terms, but no law required such a limit. But World War II had broken out in Europe, and Americans, fearing the war would soon involve them, wanted proven leadership in the White House. Roosevelt's leadership during the war was so strong that in 1944 the unprecedented happened again; Roosevelt was elected a fourth time. Two months into his 4th term, and just four months before the war ended, Roosevelt died. A stunned nation mourned the loss of the man who had led the country through two of the most serious crises of its history.

AMAZING TRUTH!

The Invisible Wheelchair

Because of Polio, Roosevelt could not walk, and had to use a wheelchair. However, he did not want Americans to know this, and he worked hard to keep this fact a secret. He did not allow photographs to be taken of him in the wheelchair, and very few Americans knew that their four-term president was paralyzed.

Ronald Reagan
(1911-2004)
The Great Communicator

Ronald Reagan was born in 1911 in Tampico, Illinois. In college, he was the kind of person who seemed to be good at everything. He played football, acted in plays, was president of the student body, and was captain of the swim team. In 1937, Reagan went to Hollywood to audition for a job as an actor. He was so impressive that Warner Brothers signed him to a seven-year contract. He immediately went to work, starring in his first film, *Love Is On The Air*. He became a major movie star, and eventually appeared in over 50 films. However, in 1942, he was called into active army duty for World War II.

After the war, Reagan became interested in politics. In 1964, he gave a speech supporting Republican presidential candidate, Barry Goldwater. The speech was so electrifying, people realized Reagan would be an excellent political candidate himself. As a result, he ran for governor of California in 1966 and won. During his eight years as governor of California, Reagan established himself as a major Republican leader. He worked to cut government spending and decrease the role of government in the everyday lives of Californians.

In 1980, Reagan was elected president. At the time of his election, America faced many difficult challenges. The standoff between the U.S. and the Soviet Union, known as the Cold War was in its fifth decade. Both nations were spending billions of dollars on weapons and defense in order to keep up with each other. Unemployment was near 10 percent, and inflation was choking the American economy. Reagan provided the bold leadership the nation desperately needed. Because of his ability to make great speeches, he was often called "The Great Communicator." His plan for the economy called for lower taxes and lower government spending, to free up cash so Americans could invest and spend as they needed. This approach worked! Jobs were created and inflation came down.

Reagan also helped bring an end to the Cold War with the Soviets using his speech-making ability. In 1987, he gave a famous speech in Berlin in which he spoke directly to the leader of the Soviets. "Mr. Gorbachev, tear down this wall." The Soviet Union was a Communist nation where people had very few rights. The Berlin Wall was part of a dividing line between free and communist countries called the Iron Curtain. By asking the Soviet leader to tear down the wall, Reagan was urging the Soviets to grant freedom to the many Communist nations they controlled. In 1989, the wall began to come down, and by 1991 the Soviet Union became the Russian Federation or Russia.

By the time Reagan left office, he had restored American economic power and re-established American military confidence around the world. His policies created thousands of jobs and made America, once again, a proud, patriotic, and prosperous nation.

AMAZING TRUTH!

The Great Commentator?
After graduating from college, Reagan got a job as a sports radio announcer in Iowa. He did play-by-play broadcasts of University of Iowa football games, and announced Chicago Cubs games.

Louis Armstrong
(1901-1971)
"Satchmo"

Louis Armstrong was born in New Orleans, Louisiana, surrounded by the sounds of jazz music. He marveled at the popular musicians and sang with his friends on the streets for nickels and pennies. Then on New Year's Eve of 1913, he was arrested for firing a gun in the air in celebration. He was sentenced to the Colored Waifs Home where he was taught to play the cornet. He was imitating the leading jazz players, including King Oliver.

BIGGEST EVENT OF THE SEASON! Week of July 21-27

OUR OWN

Louis Armstrong

World-Famous Trumpet Soloist And His Orchestra

AT THE

GOLDEN DRAGON

SUNDAY MATINEE - 4 to 8 P. M.
Admission 75c., tax 12c., total 87c.

SUNDAY NIGHT 10 P. M. to 3 A. M.
Admission $1.00, tax 15c, total $1.15

MONDAY NIGHT, 10 P. M. to 3 A. M.
Admission $1.00, tax 15c total $1.15

Balance of Weekly Schedule

FREE! Tuesday and Thursday FREE!
RHAPSODIANS ORCHESTRA

SATURDAY NIGHT
Four Pals Dance- Music by Kid Clayton's Orch.
ADMISSION 20c.

Cocktail Hour Daily 4 to 9 P. M.   All Cocktails 10c

Tickets on sa
Astoria Re
Eureka Pharmac
For quic

Oliver was so impressed with Armstrong that he invited him to join his band in Chicago. Armstrong married the band's pianist, Lil Hardin, who encouraged Armstrong to go solo. He soon played with big orchestras and created his famous "Armstrong Hot Five and Hot Seven" recordings during the mid-1920s.

Armstrong then switched to the trumpet, and no one could match his technique, his sense of harmony, or his gift for melody. His musical energy flowed through his horn, and the recordings were milestones in jazz music. Armstrong moved to New York and began using his gift for improvisation with more popular tunes from composers like Fats Waller, Duke Ellington, Hoagy Carmichael, and Irving Berlin. He also began using his gravel voice to sing and perform vocal improvisations called scat singing (a style he helped invent).

Armstrong went on to appear in movies and toured almost constantly, growing jazz music wherever he went. He was an ambassador of jazz music, and his efforts turned jazz music from a passing fad to a real art form.

AMAZING TRUTH!

Hello, Satchelmouth!

Louis Armstrong is often known by his nickname, "Satchmo," which was short for Satchelmouth. As he played, his cheeks would inflate like a balloon, looking much like a bag or satchel. A London magazine editor used the shorter version in 1932, and Armstrong liked it so much he used it for an album title.

ELVIS PRESLEY
(1935-1977)
THE KING

Elvis Aaron Presley was born in a humble home in Tupelo, Mississippi, during the Great Depression. His parents moved a lot, but they attended church regularly where gospel music became a major influence. Presley won a talent show at the age of 10, and a year after graduating from high school, he recorded his first song. A year after that, Presley had his first number-one hit with "Heartbreak Hotel," his first number-one album, *Elvis Presley*, and a movie deal with Paramount Pictures. Soon Presley seemed to be everywhere – at the movies, on the radio, and on a host of television programs. But like any American boy of his age, he was drafted into military service, where he spent a year and a half in Germany. Upon completion of his service in the army, Presley picked up where he left off and continued to act in movies such as *Blue Hawaii* (1961) and *Viva Las Vegas* (1964).

In 1968, when his popularity seemed to be shrinking, Presley performed in his first television special and showed the world what a musical force he was. Around the same time, he also got married and had a baby girl. Things seemed to be looking up for the King of rock-and-roll!

Sadly, within a few short years, his marriage fell apart. Presley was also battling an addiction to prescription drugs and a weight problem. Still, he remained popular with the public until his death from heart failure in 1977 at his home (called Graceland) in Memphis, Tennessee. Fans still flock to Graceland today (now a museum), and his 18 number-one-hit songs are classics that still have people a rockin' and a rollin'!

AMAZING TRUTH!

Twin Kings?

Believe it or not, Elvis Presley was actually an identical twin. His brother, Jesse, was born 35 minutes before Elvis, but he was stillborn (died before birth). Would there have been two Kings of rock-and-roll? We'll never know.

SUSAN B. ANTHONY
(1820-1906)
CRUSADER FOR WOMEN'S RIGHTS

Susan B. Anthony was born in Massachusetts to a Quaker family. They had many strong beliefs. They opposed slavery and supported the temperance movement. The temperance movement was a group of people who wanted to ban the drinking of alcohol.

Like her parents, Anthony also became involved in the anti-slavery and temperance movements. One day in 1852, Anthony was not allowed to speak at a temperance conference because she was a woman. So she banded together with her friend, Elizabeth Cady Stanton, and together they began to fight for women's rights, especially the right to vote.

In 1868, she created a weekly newspaper called *Revolution* to make people aware of women's issues. She also joined with Stanton and founded the National Woman's Suffrage Association. She wanted to fight for the right to vote in court, so she attempted to vote for the president in 1872. She was arrested, but there was no court case, only a fine.

That didn't stop her, though. She kept giving lectures and speeches on women's rights and even published a series of books on the history of women's rights. Though she died in 1906, other women continued the cause. Finally, in 1920, Anthony's work paid off and the 19th amendment to the Constitution passed. Women were allowed to vote!

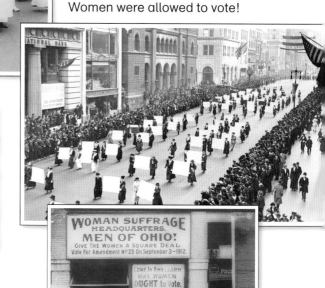

AMAZING TRUTH!

No Toys!

As a child, Susan B. Anthony rarely played with toys. Her father actually forbade toys or "amusements" in the house so the children could focus on more spiritual matters.

Dr. Martin Luther King, Jr.
(1929-1968)
American Dreamer

Martin Luther King, Jr. was born in 1929 in Atlanta, Georgia. After graduating from college, he went to a seminary to learn to become a pastor. After receiving a Ph.D. from a Boston seminary in 1954, he became the pastor of Dexter Avenue Baptist Church in Montgomery, Alabama. His $4,200-a-year salary made him the highest paid African American pastor in the city. Nineteen months after starting the job, King's life was changed forever when a 43-year-old African American seamstress, named Rosa Parks, was arrested in Montgomery. She had broken a city law by refusing to give up her bus seat to a white man. To protest this injustice, Dr. King organized a year-long boycott of city busses. Thanks to his leadership, the boycott was successful, and the American Civil Rights movement had begun.

As a result of his leadership in the Montgomery Bus Boycott, Dr. King became the leader of the Civil Rights Movement. For the next 12 years, Dr. King traveled the nation working to change America into a place where black people could enjoy the same basic privileges as white people. As he worked for change, King used his pulpit to preach a message of love and non-violent protest. He urged his followers to conduct themselves with dignity and to meet hatred with love. In the 1960s, American cities exploded with anger and violence as African Americans demanded justice, and white groups like the Ku Klux Klan worked to keep things the way they had been. King was arrested over 30 times during this period, as many southern leaders did not welcome the change he promoted.

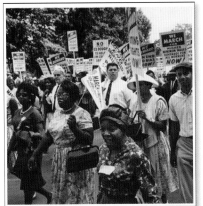

In 1968, the garbage workers of Memphis went on strike. Dr. King flew there to lead a peaceful march through the city on behalf of the workers. In the evening of April 4th, as King stood on the balcony outside his hotel room, he was struck in the head by a rifle bullet. Escaped convict, James Earl Ray, took the shot from a bathroom window of a nearby boarding house. The bullet struck King in the head, severing an artery in his neck. Within seconds, he was dead. Americans reacted in outrage and despair. Rioting broke out in over 150 cities, and over 50 people died in the violence that night. The greatest light of the 1960s had been tragically snuffed out.

 AMAZING TRUTH!

Golden Child

King was a very intelligent child. By the time he was five years old he talked as if he were an adult. When he was 15 years old, his teachers felt he had learned all that high school had to offer, so he enrolled in college. He graduated from college when he was only 19.

ALVIN C. YORK
(1887-1964)
THE SHOOTER

Alvin C. York was born in 1887 and grew up on a farm in Tennessee. He learned how to shoot a rifle from his father, and since the family hunted in order to eat, being good at shooting was important. York was particularly skilled at shooting wild turkeys. He would attend country "turkey shoots" where he would win the contests by shooting a turkey through the head.

When America entered WWI in 1917, four million young men were drafted into the army, and York was one of them. He asked to be excused from duty because he didn't think it was right to kill people, even in war. However, the army required him to serve anyway.

Once he was in the army, his company commander was able to explain to York that sometimes wars have to be fought in order to stop evil rulers from taking the lives of innocent people. Once York understood what World War I was about, he was ready to do his duty.

York and his unit arrived in France on the Western Front in the spring of 1918. He finally saw his first real action in October in the Battle of the Argonne Forrest. At this time, York was a corporal, a low rank in the army.

During the battle, on October 8, York's company was attempting to advance through a valley in order to capture a railroad line. The valley was ringed with German artillery and machine gun nests, and the American soldiers were pinned down under a withering fire. York's lieutenant selected 17 men to back out of the valley and go around the left side of the battlefield in order to get behind the enemy. As York and the other men hiked through the forest, they entered a clearing where about 30 Germans were sitting down eating breakfast. The Germans put their hands up to surrender.

As the American troops began to disarm this large group of prisoners, Germans in the hills above yelled to the prisoners to hit the ground and then opened fire from machine gun nests. Most of the 17 Americans were killed or wounded immediately, but York was not hit. Using his rifle, York began to shoot the German gunners as they raised their heads to see him. He did this in the same way he used to shoot turkeys as a boy back in Tennessee. York killed 15 Germans. Next, seven Germans charged straight at York, running downhill toward him. York had his Colt pistol dangling from his finger and now began to use it. He shot each of the charging Germans, taking out the one in the rear first, and then working forward, so that none of the Germans knew that his comrades were going down. This too was a turkey shooting technique.

After seeing such a display of bravery and marksmanship, now over 100 overwhelmed Germans in the area surrendered to York. As he marched these prisoners out of the woods, more Germans joined the group. When he returned to the safety of the American lines, he had 132 prisoners with him. York was awarded the Medal of Honor for his bravery in battle that day.

AMAZING TRUTH!

Perfect Shot

After York turned in his 132 German prisoners, he was asked how many times he had fired his weapons. He reported that he had shot 28 bullets that day. The next day, the site of his heroics was inspected, and 28 dead Germans were found.

AUDIE MURPHY
(1924-1971)
AMERICAN HERO

Because he was the most highly-decorated American soldier of World War II, Audie Murphy was a very special person. But in fact, he was always a very special person. As a young boy he and his nine brothers and sisters found themselves without a father, so Murphy dropped out of school in the 5th grade to get a job to help support the family. Later, when the Japanese bombed Pearl Harbor in 1941, he was only 16 but desperately wanted to go fight for his country. The Army required enlistees to be 18, so his sister altered his birth certificate. It worked. Just after his 17th birthday, the U.S. Army enlisted him in the infantry.

Murphy first saw action in Sicily and Italy in 1943 and 1944, and distinguished himself as an outstanding soldier. He received multiple promotions and medals due to his bravery in combat. However, the bravery he showed on a battlefield in France in 1945 set him apart forever. On the outskirts of a French town called Holtzwihr, six German tanks and 250 German soldiers attacked Lieutenant Murphy and his men. Outnumbered, Murphy ordered his men to fall back into the woods while he slowed the Germans with covering fire. He emptied his rifle, Then, as he prepared to withdraw, he spotted a burning American tank destroyer with a .50 caliber machine gun on it. Ignoring the danger, he jumped on the vehicle and turned its large machine gun against the Germans. Wounded and bleeding, Murphy finally jumped off of the tank destroyer moments before it exploded. His actions stopped a German tank unit and saved the lives of his entire unit.

For his actions that day in France, Murphy won the Medal of Honor, America's highest military award. Murphy showed similar valor on other occasions, and by the time the war ended, he had collected 32 decorations in all. These included two Bronze Stars, two Silver Stars, the Distinguished Service Cross, and three Purple Hearts. No other American won so many honors during the war.

After the war, Murphy became a Hollywood film star, appearing in over 40 films. His most successful film was called *To Hell and Back*, and it was the true story of his actions in World War II. He played himself. Sadly, he died in 1971 when his private plane crashed in Virginia. He is buried at Arlington National Cemetery near Washington, D.C., and his grave is the second most visited in the cemetery, after John F. Kennedy's.

AMAZING TRUTH!

Tank Killer

Murphy is credited with killing at least 250 Germans during World War II, and destroying six tanks.

THEODORE ROOSEVELT
(1858-1919)
THE ROUGH RIDER

Theodore Roosevelt is probably the most fascinating of all American presidents. Taking office in 1901 after the shooting death of William McKinley, he was the youngest U.S. president ever at age 42. He was a speed-reader, going through one book each day. He wrote over 20 books himself, and he also wrote over 150,000 letters. Once in Milwaukee, he was shot in the chest but insisted on giving his planned speech before going to the hospital. He also personally led men (the Rough Riders) in battle during the Spanish American War. His is the only modern face among the four presidents on Mt. Rushmore.

He absolutely loved nature and animals. He went deep into Africa on hunting safaris, and his fishing expeditions took him into uncharted areas of the Amazon. Many of the wild animals he shot are still on display in the Smithsonian Institute today. And he, more than any other president, is responsible for the creation of America's beautiful national parks and wildlife preserves. He started the National Park Service, and set aside 40 million acres of land that will be forever preserved as a natural habitat for plants and animals.

Roosevelt fell in love with the study of animals when he was just a child. This interest began when he was seven when he saw a dead seal displayed at a dock in New York City. It had been killed in the harbor, and he came to see it every day. He bought a pocket ruler and measured the seal's dimensions. After begging for it, he was finally given the animal's skull, which he preserved in his collection, which began now.

Theodore Roosevelt came from a fabulously wealthy family. For example, when he was a student at Harvard, the university's president made a salary of $5,000 a year, but Teddy's annual allowance was $8,000. But even though he was wealthy, Teddy cared deeply about helping people in need. As a politician, he was known as a Progressive, meaning he worked to make life better for poor and underprivileged Americans. He worked hard to get young children out of factories and into schools, to help immigrants get jobs, and to improve living conditions in the overcrowded slums of American cities.

AMAZING TRUTH!

A Very Cuddly Bear

Even though Roosevelt loved to hunt animals, he did not shoot everything he saw. Once, while hunting in Mississippi in 1902, he cornered a bear cub and allowed it live. This story captured the imagination of Americans, and led to the creation of a brand new toy, the Teddy Bear.

JOHN F. KENNEDY
(1917-1963)
YOUNG STATESMAN

John F. Kennedy (or JFK, as he was known) was born in Massachusetts in 1917 and one of nine children from a prominent Irish American family. He attended Harvard University in Cambridge, Massachusetts, and then joined the Navy during World War II.

In 1960, Kennedy ran for president against Richard Nixon, and the election was one of the closest in U.S. history. JFK won by just 112,000 out of more than 68 million votes cast. At age 43, Kennedy was the youngest man ever elected President. As he took office, Kennedy called for Americans to "ask not what your country can do for you; ask what you can do for your country." He then called on the nations of the world to "ask not what America can do for you, but what together we can do for the freedom of man."

Though he called on world leaders to seek peace and tolerance, he was often forced to defend America from the growing military build-up by the Soviet Union, which came to be known as the Cold War. In the 1962 Cuban Missile Crisis, JFK used a naval blockade to stop nuclear missiles from being shipped to communist Cuba. Kennedy also announced the U.S. plans to send a man to the moon before the end of the decade (which happened in 1969). Sadly, Kennedy would never see that goal realized. Two bullets from an assassin's rifle struck him as he toured Dallas in a limousine in 1963. He was rushed to nearby Parkland Memorial Hospital, but doctors declared him dead just minutes after his arrival.

AMAZING TRUTH!

Shipwrecked!

Seventeen years before being elected president, Kennedy became famous as a hero of World War II. He was the skipper of *Patrol Torpedo Boat 109* (*PT-109*), and in August 1943, a massive Japanese destroyer actually drove through the ship, cutting it in two. Two crewmen died in the wreck, but 11, including Kennedy, managed to swim to a deserted island. Kennedy's leadership and swimming ability saved the lives of many of his men. Rescued six days later, the story appeared in nearly every newspaper in the country.

THE ATHLETES

MIA HAMM
(1972-)
SOCCER QUEEN

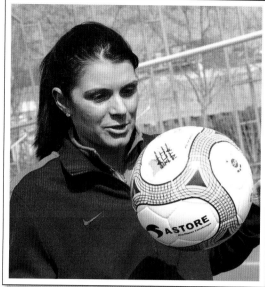

Mariel Margaret Hamm was born in Selma, Alabama, in 1972. Her mother, a ballet dancer, gave her the nickname "Mia" in honor of her mother's dance mentor, Mia Slavenska. She's been called Mia ever since. Of course, it was a strange nickname for a child born with partial club feet (a condition where the feet are turned inwards). To correct the defect, she wore special shoes. But that didn't slow down little Mia. According to her father, Mia saw someone playing soccer when she was 18 months old. She ran over and kicked the ball!

As a child, Hamm learned to play soccer while living in Italy (her father was an U.S. Air Force pilot). It was clear that she had a gift for the game. She went on to play for the U.S. Women's Soccer Team at the age of 15. She entered college at 17 and helped the University of North Carolina win 4 national championships. Hamm also played on the U.S. World Cup team with Michelle Akers, Brandi Chastain, and Kristine Lilly in 1991. The World Cup is like the World Series of soccer. It is governed by an international soccer group called FIFA (Fédération Internationale de Football Association). The U.S. Women's Soccer Team won the first FIFA Women's World Cup in 1991, making Hamm (19 at the time) the youngest player to ever win the World Cup. The win turbo-charged the growth of soccer in America! Soccer teams and leagues took hold like never before.

When Hamm and the members of the team played in the 1999 World Cup at the Rose Bowl in California, over 90,000 people attended the game making it the best-attended women's sporting event in history! To top it off, they won their 2nd World Cup, making them one of the most dominant teams in the sport. Year after year, the team went on to win Olympic Gold Medals (1996, 2004) and made the semi-finals of every FIFA Women's World Cup ever since. Hamm and teammate Michelle Akers were both put on the list of FIFA's 125 greatest living soccer players. They were the only women and the only Americans to make the list. Hamm was also named the FIFA World Player of the Year in 2001 and 2002. Today, Hamm enjoys helping people through her Mia Hamm Foundation that studies bone marrow and blood diseases like the one that killed her brother, Garrett, in 1997. She is also mother to twin girls and likes to encourage kids everywhere to follow their dreams and play soccer!

AMAZING TRUTH!

TOUCHDOWN!

Mia Hamm knows how to find a net, but soccer wasn't her only sport growing up. She actually played football in junior high school (middle school) for Notre Dame Catholic School in Wichita Falls, Texas. Hamm played split end and defensive back for the team.

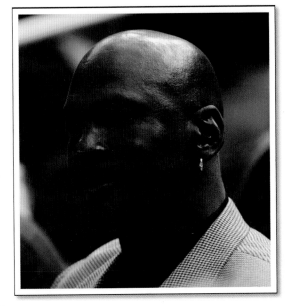

MICHAEL JORDAN
(1963-)
HIS AIRNESS

Michael Jordan was born in Brooklyn, New York, but moved to Wilmington on the coast of North Carolina as a toddler. There his competitive spirit soared, playing football, basketball and baseball. Soon basketball became Jordan's focus, earning him a scholarship to the University of North Carolina and honors as a McDonald's All-American.

His rookie year in college brought even more honors as he was named the Atlantic Coast Conference (ACC) Freshman of the Year. The next year, in 1982, he made the winning jump shot in the NCAA championship game against Georgetown (led by future pro-star, Patrick Ewing). The win was a major turning point in Jordan's career, and two years later, in 1984, he left school to join the NBA, playing for the Chicago Bulls (though he finished his college degree the next year).

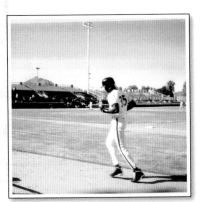

Jordan made an instant splash in the league, earning the Rookie-of-the-Year Award and making his first of 14 appearances in the All-Star Game. He took the Bulls to their first appearance in the NBA playoffs, but it wasn't until 1991 that he led them to the championship…three years in a row (known as a three-peat)!

When his father was killed in a robbery, Jordan stepped away from the court and decided to play baseball for the minor league team, Birmingham Barons. The time away seemed to energize Jordan, who returned to the Bulls and helped them win three more championships before retiring again. Of course, the pictures of Jordan sailing through the air and dunking the ball from the foul line live on in the minds of basketball fans everywhere.

AMAZING TRUTH!

Too Short To Compete?

Michael Jordan tried out for his high school varsity basketball team his sophomore year. He didn't make it. The reason? They thought he was too short to compete (he was 5 feet 11 inches tall). He proved them wrong with several 40-point games on the junior varsity team, and he grew four inches over the summer. The next year he made varsity.

SANDRA DAY O'CONNOR
(1930-)
SUPREME COURT JUSTICE

Born in El Paso, Texas, Sandra Day O'Connor grew up on an Arizona cattle ranch but stayed with her grandmother in El Paso for most of her schooling. She attended Stanford University where she received a degree in economics in 1950, and then attended Stanford's law school.

Though she was a star-student in law school, no law firm in California would hire her because she was a woman. So she started out in public service as an attorney for San Mateo County, California, and later became the assistant attorney general of Arizona. After a few years, she was appointed to the Arizona legislature by Republican Governor Jack Williams.

She was re-elected for two more terms and became the first female majority leader in a state legislature. Returning to court, O'Connor was elected to the Maricopa County Superior Court in Arizona. Later, Democratic Governor Bruce Babbitt appointed her to the Arizona Court of Appeals. Then in 1981, President Ronald Reagan nominated her for the U.S. Supreme Court. She was confirmed by an unheard-of unanimous, bi-partisan vote of 99-0 by the U.S. Senate.

Though O'Connor often voted along with other conservative justices in key court cases, O'Connor was the deciding vote against overturning Roe vs. Wade, (the case that made abortion legal). Yet she always used the law and the U.S. Constitution as guiding documents when it came to cases. But when her husband became ill with Alzheimer's disease, she decided to retire to spend more time with him and her family. In recognition of her achievements, President Barack Obama awarded her the Presidential Medal of Freedom in 2009. And she continues to inspire future generations!

AMAZING TRUTH!

Supreme Coincidence?

While in law school, Sandra Day O'Connor wrote for the *Stanford Law Review*. She briefly dated the presiding editor-in-chief and future U.S. Supreme Court Chief Justice William Rehnquist.

BARACK OBAMA
(1961-)
GAME CHANGER

Barack Hussein Obama, Jr., was born in Hawaii to a mother from the Midwest and a father from Kenya. The couple had fallen in love and married while at the University of Hawaii, but after two years they separated and later divorced. Obama only saw his father once more in 1971. He often

wondered what it might have been like if his father had stayed, and he wrote about it in his best-selling book, *Dreams of My Father*.

His mother later remarried, and they moved to Indonesia for a few years then back to Hawaii where Obama lived with his grandparents. His college years were spent in California, then New York where he attended Columbia University and graduated in 1983.

After graduating from Columbia University, Obama spent time in Chicago as a community organizer helping low-income residents. In this role, he realized that in order to help make the change he thought was necessary, he needed to become more familiar with the law. Determined to act, he went to Harvard Law School where he became the first African American editor of the *Harvard Law Review*.

Five years after graduation, Obama ran for the Illinois State Senate and won. A few years later, in 2004, Obama was elected to the U.S. Senate. He was the third African American elected to the Senate since the Civil War. His star continued to rise as he ran for president of the United States. When he won the election, he became the first African American president, forever shattering the race barrier. An electric sense of hope and change filled the nation as Obama took office in 2009, and his legacy is still being written today!

AMAZING TRUTH!

Hey, Barry!

Barack Obama wasn't always called Barack.

Growing up he was known as "Barry." It wasn't until

college that he insisted on being called Barack.

GLOSSARY

Abolitionist – A person who worked to bring an end to (abolish) slavery in America in the years before the Civil War.

Alzheimer's Disease – A disease that gradually takes away your ability to remember things including where you are and how to talk, eventually causing the person with the disease to die in most cases.

Almanac(k) – A yearly book that contains information about the movement of the sun, stars, and the moon, as well as, the seasons and bits of wisdom or knowledge.

Amateur – Someone who is new or has very little experience doing something.

Artery – a large blood vessel that carries blood from the heart to the rest of the body.

Bi-Partisan – Something that involves people from two political parties, like Democrats and Republicans.

Bleeding Kansas – A series of violent events in mid-1850s in Kansas in which over 200 people died. The fighting took place between people who wanted Kansas to become a slave state and people who wanted it to be a free state.

Cold War – Period between 1945 and 1991, in which the United States and the Soviet Union fought for control of various countries around the world.

Communism – An economic theory that calls for shared property in a classless society where all activity is controlled by a totalitarian dictator.

Conservative – Someone who believes in small government, low taxes, and as few rules as possible.

Congress – The House of Representatives and the Senate; the elected, law-making group of men and women from each state who create national laws.

Congressman/woman – An elected man or woman from the U.S. House of Representatives.

Cornet – An instrument similar to a trumpet with a softer, more mellow sound and shorter metal tubing.

Diplomat – Someone who represents a country to other countries or governments, often helping both countries to get along with each other.

Draft – A law that forces people to join the army, usually during a time of war.

Editor – Someone who runs a newspaper or magazine and makes corrections to other writers' work.

Electoral Vote – System for electing the U.S. president in which each state is assigned a certain number of electoral votes based on how many people live in the state. If a person wins the majority of a state's votes, he then receives all of the state's electoral votes.

Governor – The leader of a state or territory.

House of Representatives – An elected, law-making group of men and women that is based on the number of people living in each area. This allows areas or states with more people to have the most votes on new laws.

John Brown – Pre-Civil War abolitionist who led a violent raid on the U.S. arsenal at Harper's Ferry, Virginia, in 1859. His raid failed and he was hanged, but he brought attention to the anti-slavery issue.

Inflation – A rise in the prices of consumer goods. When inflation takes place, the value of money goes down and things cost more.

Lab – Short for laboratory; a place where experiments are done.

Law Firm – A group of lawyers who do business.

Legislature – An elected group of representatives who vote on laws in a republic.

Low-Income Residents – People who live in a certain area that do not make very much money.

Markswoman/man – Someone who is very good at shooting and hitting targets.

Massacre – The unnecessary killing of large numbers of people.

Mob – A group of people often coming together to protest or hurt someone or something they don't like.

Mt. Rushmore – Massive monument carved into a mountain in South Dakota. The monument has the faces of Presidents Washington, Jefferson, Lincoln and Theodore Roosevelt.

Monopoly – When one company has no competition for a product and controls the market for that item or service.

Paralyzed – Medical condition in which a person cannot move all, or part, of their body.

Patent – A law that stops people from copying other inventors' inventions and making money from it without permission.

Plantation – A large farm that uses many workers or slaves who often live on the plantation.

Polio – A viral disease typically attacking children and young adults that results in paralysis, deformity, and muscular weakness.

Seminary – A special school that teaches people about religion so they can become a minister, or pastor, of a Christian church.

Senate – An elected, law-making group of men and women where each area has the same number of representatives. This allows smaller areas or states to have an equal vote to the bigger areas or states on new laws.

Showman – Someone who organizes and puts on shows to entertain people.

Skipper – A captain or commander of a ship.

Soviet Union – A group of Communist nations led by Russia that existed between 1922 and 1991.

State Legislature – An elected, law-making group of people in a state normally made up of a house of representative and a senate. Similar to the U.S. Congress.

Statesman – An experienced politician or law-maker, usually respected by others.

Steel – a metal; a form of iron that has been changed so that it is lighter and stronger.

Stogie – Slang term for cigar; a roll of dried tobacco made for smoking.

Suffrage – The right to vote in elections.

Tank Destroyer – An armored vehicle similar to a tank, that is made to be very good at destroying enemy tanks.

Tax – Money that, by law, must be given to the government to pay for government expenses such as roads, schools, police, firefighting.

Telegraph – A message sent or received using a machine that allowed messages to be sent with Morse Code over long distances using electricity and wires.

Term – The length of time an elected representative serves.

Unalienable – Something that cannot be taken away or given to another person.

Unprecedented – Something that has never happened before or that has no previous example.

Valedictorian – A student in school who graduates with the highest grades of anyone in their class.

Vertical Integration – When many businesses within one company work together on the different steps of making a product.

INDEX